WE ARE LIMITED, EVERYTHING ELSE IS A LIE

WE ARE LIMITED, EVERYTHING ELSE IS A LIE

PRAVEEN VATTAPPARAMBATH

Ardra Publishers

CONTENTS

You are limited
Everything else is a lie

PRAVEEN VATTAPPARAMBATH
Cover Graphics: Dr.Aarsha Arjun
Copyright © 2023 Praveen Vattapparambath
All rights reserved.
ISBN: 9789360129767

ACKNOWLEDGMENTS

To my dear wife Veena, who has been my pillar of strength and unwavering support throughout my journey as a writer. Without your love, encouragement, and patience, this book would not have been possible.

To my best friend, Dr. Mayalekshmi, who has been with me through thick and thin, and whose invaluable feedback and encouragement have been instrumental in shaping me as a writer.

To my mentor, Ceejo Thomas, whose guidance, insights, and expertise have been invaluable in shaping my writing and publishing journey. Thank you for sharing your wisdom and for believing in me.

And to my gangs of psychology – Bini, Latha and Aarsha who have stood by me, cheered me on, and offered their unwavering support in countless ways.

This book is dedicated to my family, each one of you, and I hope it brings as much joy and inspiration to you as you have brought to me.

preface

Throughout my life, I've been drawn to the world of motivational books and classes, seeking that much-needed spark to propel me towards success. I invested my time and hard-earned money into these resources, hoping to find lasting motivation and a surefire path to achievement. However, the reality I discovered was far from what I had expected.

Many of these motivational teachings promised a quick fix, a miraculous transformation where dreams come true effortlessly. They preached the idea that with enough belief in oneself, anything is possible, and giving up should never be an option. While these messages were undoubtedly inspiring, I soon realized their underlying flaw - they painted an unrealistic picture of life.

Life, as we all know, is a series of ups and downs, filled with challenges and obstacles that often stand in our way. Despite our best efforts, there will be times when our goals remain unattained, and dreams may seem out of reach. It is in these moments that we must confront the disparity between the idealistic notions fed to us and the harsh realities we encounter.

This book is not here to condemn your habits or dismiss all motivational classes as ineffective. Instead, it aims to bring you back to earth, to illuminate the realities of life and foster realistic expectations. It's about acknowledging that failure is an inevitable part of our journey, and that stumbling along the way does not signify the end of the road.

Within these pages, I aim to guide you in embracing failure as an opportunity for growth, learning valuable lessons from your missteps, and discovering the resilience to keep forging ahead. This book is not about handing you a prepackaged formula for success. Instead, it empowers you to find your own unique motivation, to create a path tailored to your aspirations and circumstances.

So, let us embark on this journey together. Let us explore the intricacies of motivation and success, recognizing that true fulfilment lies not in unrealistic promises, but in our ability to navigate the complexities of life with determination, adaptability, and an unwavering belief in ourselves.

Lies, Lies and Lies

Credits @ Dr.Aroha Arjun

Lies, Lies and Lies

Motivational Speaker: Alright folks, get ready to unleash the power of limitlessness! Are you ready to break through your barriers and achieve your dreams?

Mr. Victim: Woohoo! I'm feeling invincible! Ain't no stopping me now, I'm on fire! I'm like the superhero Jesus!

Motivational Speaker: That's the spirit! With the power of limitlessness, you can conquer anything and everything. No challenge is too big, no obstacle is too tough. You're a force to be reckoned with, my friend!

Mr. Victim: You got that right, buddy! I'm gonna soar higher than an eagle, run faster than a cheetah, and swim deeper than a dolphin! Nothing can hold me back now!

This story narrates a real-life experience that a friend of the speaker recently shared. The friend was conducting an online interview for a job opening in his company when he noticed a pile of papers hanging in the background of the candidate's video feed. Curious, the friend inquired about the papers, and the candidate revealed that they were filled with motivational quotes from famous speakers in the field.

The candidate went on to explain that they would read these quotes out loud every day and that it gave them a sense of inspiration and motivation. They believed that constantly reading and imitating these passages would enhance their immense talent and enable them to achieve anything they set their minds to.

However, the candidate's performance during the interview was un-impressive, suggesting that they were unprepared for the questions or not qualified for the job. Despite their belief in the power of motivational quotes, they were unable to back it up with practical skills and knowledge.

You know that book on your shelf that you bought thinking it would help you become a total boss? And have you heard of the "Conspiring Universe" theory? It's like the ultimate conspiracy theory for young people these days. Our writers possess a rare talent for weaving together the threads of fate and happenstance into intricate conspiracy theories.

Maybe it's one of those books that talks about motivation and engi-neering your life for success. They're like a big, tempting bag of candy for anyone feeling hopeless or lost in life. It is often said that books have been a source of inspiration for us, providing us with life stories of great people and interesting anecdotes filled with humor. They also play a significant role in teaching us that failure and exhaustion should not be viewed as negative experiences.

For those who find themselves languishing in the depths of despair, the allure of "Positive Visions" - be it through books, classes or lectures - is a siren's song that promises to lead one to the shores of success. Yet, it is not my intention to condemn these teachings outright. It is only by gauging their efficacy against the harsh realities of life that we can deem them to be truly beneficial.

But here's the thing - not all of those books are gonna be winners. Some of them might even take you further away from what's actually possible in the real world. Like, do you really need to be the next Bill

Gates to be considered successful? And is success even guaranteed in the first place?

It is a common misconception that success can be achieved simply by emulating the actions of those who have already succeeded. This belief is particularly appealing to those who have not achieved success themselves and may harbor feelings of envy towards those who have. In reality, success is a complex and multifaceted phenomenon that cannot be reduced to a simple formula. However, the desire to seek out and celebrate success stories is a natural human tendency and serves as the basis for many of the success strategies and motivational messages we encounter.

A lot of lies are being distributed around us, prepared to influence and make people believe by mixing the unconscious mind, sub-conscious mind and conscious mind with the accompaniment of psychology. It is not that all this is unscientific, but that all these are used to boost sales and thus we are doomed to fall prey to these colored lies. Half-truths are often more dangerous than lies.

Let me give you an example. If I were to say that an elephant flew the way I'm coming, you'd probably think I'm crazy and dismiss it. But if I were to say "John and I were startled to see an elephant fly over our heads while we were talking about an accident that happened yester-day," you might be more inclined to believe me. Especially if you know John and the accident that happened yesterday.

And that's how lies work on us, my friends. They're like little stories that tap into our unconscious, sub-conscious, and conscious minds, and before we know it, we're hooked. So, the next time someone tries to sell you something, or tells you a story that seems too good to be true, remember this: half-truths are often more dangerous than lies.

Do you believe that what was said is all untrue? It is actually written with the understanding that unscientific alien theories should be regarded as lies. For instance, personal experiences and anecdotes are often presented as a theory in motivational speeches. For example, let's consider a millionaire who only has a basic education and who, due to his teacher's disrespect, dropped out of school and went into business, ultimately achieving success. Can we call this a lie? No, it is true. So far, there is no problem. However, if this were presented as a theory and accepted to the extent that academic education is deemed irrelevant, the outcome of applying a mind with limited abilities to work without knowledge could be very disastrous instead of empowering. It's important to recognize that personal anecdotes and motivational stories can be inspiring and provide valuable lessons, but they should not be presented as factual evidence to support grand claims or theories. It's also crucial to remember that academic education and scientific inquiry are essential for advancing our understanding of the world around us and for developing effective solutions to complex problems. Dismissing them as irrelevant or unnecessary can lead to dangerous consequences and hinder progress.

In the case of the millionaire who succeeded despite having only elementary education, it's worth examining the broader societal factors that allowed for this outcome. Was the individual's success due solely to their personal qualities, or were there systemic advantages and opportunities that helped them along the way? By considering these questions and engaging in critical   analysis, we can gain a more nuanced understanding of success and how it is achieved.

I don't like working under anyone, so I decided to become independent. Look today, I became a millionaire as a result of that decision

---

The above sentence is often used as a marketing tactic by self-proclaimed leaders who claim to have achieved financial success through entrepreneurship or other means of independent work. However, this statement can be misleading and overly simplistic. While it is true that some individuals find it more fulfilling to work independently and be their own boss, entrepreneurship and independent work require a significant amount of effort, skill, and luck. Moreover, not everyone has the resources, connections, or ideas necessary to launch a successful business venture. Therefore, suggesting that anyone can become a millionaire by simply choosing to become independent is not realistic or practical advice.

Furthermore, the idea that working within a hierarchical structure is equivalent to slavery is a gross oversimplification and ignores the benefits and opportunities that come with being part of an organization. Working within a hierarchy can provide individuals with a clear path for career growth and development, access to resources and networks, and the opportunity to learn from experienced professionals.

Finally, the use of mass hypnosis and other manipulative techniques to persuade individuals to buy into these ideas is unethical and can be harmful. It is important to critically evaluate the information presented to us and consider the potential risks and benefits of any decision we make.

It all depends on you!

Everything that happens around you does not depend on you. That is a big lie. It's not that you can't have interactions, it's important to realize that your interactions aren't everything waiting. Such lies can often only bridge the gap from confidence to overindulgence" suggests that the idea of complete control over one's life is a falsehood. It acknowledges the importance of interactions but cautions against overindulging in them.

While it is true that individuals have some degree of control over their lives, there are many external factors that can impact our experiences, such as social, economic, and environmental factors. Therefore, the idea that everything that happens around us is solely determined by our individual choices and actions is a simplification that ignores the complexity of the world we live in.

At the same time, interactions with others are important for personal and professional growth. However, it is also essential to recognize that not all interactions will lead to success or happiness. Overindulging in the belief that one's interactions are the only determinants of their success can lead to unrealistic expectations and disappointment.

It is important to strike a balance between personal responsibility and acknowledging the role of external factors in our lives. By doing so, we can make more informed decisions, set realistic goals, and be better equipped to handle challenges that come our way.

Failure is not an option.

Don't be afraid to mess up and make mistakes. Embrace failure as a natural part of the learning process, and use it as a stepping stone towards growth and success. And always remember, even if you do mess up, at least you'll have a funny story to tell later!

Many people feel that failure is unacceptable and that they must always succeed in order to be successful in life. However, this pressure to succeed can be overwhelming and lead to negative consequences such as depression, anxiety, and other psychological problems.

It's important to remember that failure is a natural part of life and the learning process. No one is perfect, and everyone makes mistakes. In fact, failure can often be a valuable learning experience that helps people grow and improve. When people are constantly pressured to succeed, they may feel like they are not good enough or that they are failures if they do not meet expectations. This can lead to feelings of depression, anxiety, and other mental health issues.

Instead of putting so much weight on success, it's important to encourage people to embrace failure as a natural part of life and to use it as an opportunity to learn and grow. When people are not afraid to fail, they are more likely to take risks and try new things, which can lead to greater success in the long run.

In short, while success is important, it's equally important to embrace failure as a natural and valuable part of life. By doing so, we can help reduce the pressure and stress that people feel to succeed, and encourage them to take risks and pursue their dreams without fear of failure.

Failure may bring tears and pain,
But it's not the end of the game.
Dust off and rise up again,
And you can fail again too.

Positive thinking can solve all your problems

We've all heard the saying that positive thinking can solve all our problems, but let's be real here - if positive thinking alone could fix everything, we wouldn't need doctors, engineers, or plumbers, we'd just need a bunch of happy-go-lucky folks with good vibes.

Positive thinking doesn't have to be grounded in reality. I mean, you could wake up every morning and recite affirmations in front of the mirror, but that won't magically solve all your problems. In fact, unrealistic positive thinking can even lead you down the wrong path.

For instance, let's say you're struggling with a financial crisis. You may start thinking positively, telling yourself that you can handle it all without breaking a sweat. Then, your thoughts may take a turn towards daydreaming about hitting the jackpot with some get-rich-quick scheme that popped into your head. But let's face it - unless you're a wizard or a fairy godmother, those dreams are nothing but distractions from reality.

In fact, unrealistic positivity can sometimes make things worse. If you focus too much on grandiose daydreams, you may lose sight of practical, achievable solutions that could actually help you get out of your financial predicament.

So, while it's great to have a positive outlook on life, it's also important to stay grounded in reality and focus on practical solutions. And if all else fails, just remember that money can't buy happiness, but it can buy chocolate, and that's pretty close.

You must always be positive and happy

While happiness is certainly an important part of life, it's unrealistic to expect to be happy all the time. Life is full of ups and downs, and it's important to embrace all of our emotions and experiences, even the difficult ones. Trying to approach life dispassionately or without emotion is not only difficult, it's also not very fulfilling.

Take the example of a love affair. While it can bring great happiness, it can also bring sadness, turmoil, and even heartbreak. These emotions are all a natural part of the experience of love. If the relationship comes to an end, it's normal to feel sad and even depressed. Trying to avoid these emotions altogether is not only impossible, it's also not healthy. It's important to acknowledge and process our emotions, even the difficult ones, in order to move forward and grow.

Ultimately, the key is to approach life with awareness and acceptance. We can't control everything that happens to us, but we can control how we respond to it. Instead of trying to avoid or suppress our emotions, we can acknowledge and accept them as a natural part of the human experience. By doing so, we can move through difficult times with more grace and resilience, and ultimately find greater fulfilment and meaning in our lives.

Furthermore, experiencing negative emotions can actually help us appreciate the positive ones more fully. Without sadness, we wouldn't appreciate happiness as much. Without disappointment, we wouldn't appreciate success as much. It's the contrast between the different emotions and experiences that make life rich and meaningful.

It's also important to remember that failure and setbacks are a natural part of any journey towards success. In fact, many successful people have experienced multiple failures before achieving their goals. The idea that we should always be succeeding and achieving is simply not realistic. Instead, we should embrace our failures and learn from them. By doing so, we can develop resilience and perseverance, which are essential qualities for achieving success in any area of life.

CHAPTER 2

Myth of limitless self

Believing in our unlimited potential means thinking that we are capable of achieving anything and everything we desire. While this mindset can be empowering, it can also lead to a scattered purpose. When we believe that we can do anything, we may find ourselves pursuing multiple goals simultaneously without a clear focus. For example, imagine someone who believes they have unlimited potential in various fields such as music, sports, and business. They may spread themselves thin by trying to excel in all of these areas simultaneously, which can hinder their overall progress and prevent them from achieving significant success in any one field.

On the other hand, when our efforts are monotonous, meaning they are focused and repetitive, we often achieve better results. Monotony allows us to concentrate our energy and attention on a specific task or skill, enabling us to become more proficient in that area. For instance, consider a musician who practices the same piece of music repeatedly. By focusing on perfecting the nuances and mastering the composition through repetitive practice, the musician can achieve a higher level of skill and deliver a more impressive performance.

When we view personality development as something to be pursued with competitive intelligence, it implies that we approach it as a competition with others. In this context, we feel the need to compare ourselves constantly, striving to outperform and surpass others in various aspects of our personality. For example, someone might focus on acquiring knowledge, skills, and achievements solely for the purpose of being better than their peers. This competitive mindset can lead to an unhealthy obsession with comparison, validation, and an insatiable need to prove oneself superior to others.

To embrace this theory easily, we must accept the idea that personality development is a competitive pursuit. However, it is important to note that such an approach may not be conducive to holistic personal growth. It can lead to a narrow focus on external validation and accomplishments, rather than nurturing and cultivating genuine personal qualities and strengths.

We humans are far from being machines. Unlike machines, we have the ability to age, experience wear and tear, and even burnout. It's not a matter of if these things will happen to us, but rather a matter of when they will occur.

Let's take aging as an example. While machines may continue to function without any significant changes for an extended period, humans go through a natural aging process. As we get older, our bodies undergo various physical and biological changes. We may notice wrinkles appearing, a decrease in energy levels, or even a few more gray hairs. It's like that moment when you realize you can't pull an all-nighter anymore without feeling the consequences the next day, unlike those trusty machines that can tirelessly work around the clock.

Another aspect is how we can break, both physically and emotionally. Machines can break down too, but the way we humans break is quite different. We may experience injuries or illnesses that require rest, treatment, or even surgery. On the emotional side, we can feel overwhelmed, stressed, or even experience a breakdown from time to time. It's like when you push yourself too hard at work and end up faceplanting into your keyboard, whereas a machine would simply shut down or display an error message.

And let's not forget about burnout. Machines can operate at a consistent level of productivity without feeling mentally or emotionally drained. But we humans are susceptible to burnout, especially when we push ourselves excessively or neglect self-care. It's like that moment when you've been working so hard that you start questioning if you're a human or a caffeinated zombie. Meanwhile, a machine would continue to churn out its tasks without needing a break or a vacation.

So, as imperfect and wonderfully human as we are, we should recognize that we have our limitations. We age, we break, and we can burnout. Embracing our humanity means understanding that it's natural for these things to happen, and it's essential to take care of ourselves along the way.

Another significant factor that aligns with the limitless self theory is the constant urge to outperform others. This drive to surpass our colleagues in the workplace or to be more noticeable than our classmates during studies becomes a prevalent human emotion throughout our lives. It's important to note that this desire is not inherently negative, as healthy competition can motivate us and push us to achieve greater things.

However, when this urge to outperform becomes excessive, it can lead to detrimental effects. When we stretch our efforts and concentration beyond our capacity or abilities, the natural process of organic growth is hindered. It's like trying to fit a square peg into a round hole – it simply doesn't work and can cause unnecessary stress and frustration.

For example, imagine a student who constantly compares themselves to their classmates and feels compelled to outshine them in every aspect of their academic performance. They may sacrifice their well-being, neglect self-care, and overload themselves with excessive studying and extracurricular activities. In this pursuit of outperforming others, they may experience heightened levels of mental stress, leading to burnout and a decline in their overall well-being.

Similarly, in the workplace, someone who constantly seeks to outshine their colleagues may become consumed by the need for recognition and validation. They may take on more responsibilities than they can handle, neglect work-life balance, and subject themselves to chronic stress. Over time, this can have adverse effects on their mental health and hinder their ability to grow and develop in a sustainable manner.

It's essential to find a balance between healthy competition and personal growth. While it's natural to have ambitions and strive for success, it's equally important to recognize our own limitations and prioritize our well-being. Embracing organic growth means allowing ourselves to develop naturally, focusing on our own progress rather than constantly comparing ourselves to others. By doing so, we can avoid becoming addicted to mental stress and foster a healthier and more sustainable approach to personal development.

Ten percent of the brain myth

The "Ten percent of the brain" myth is a popular misconception that suggests humans only utilize ten percent of their brain's capacity, leaving the remaining 90 percent untapped and unused potential. This myth has been perpetuated in various forms, including books, movies, and self-help gurus. However, it is important to note that this idea is not supported by scientific evidence.

In reality, the human brain is a highly complex and intricate organ, and all regions of the brain have specific functions and contribute to our overall cognitive abilities. Brain imaging techniques, such as functional magnetic resonance imaging (fMRI), have shown that even during rest or seemingly simple tasks, the entire brain is active to some extent.

To further debunk the myth, consider the following examples:

Language Processing: The ability to understand and produce language involves various regions of the brain. For instance, the temporal lobe is responsible for processing auditory information, while the frontal lobe plays a role in speech production. If we were only using 10 percent of our brain, it would be challenging to engage in complex language-related activities like reading, writing, and having conversations.

Motor Skills: Motor skills involve multiple brain regions working together. When you walk, run, or perform intricate movements, various parts of the brain, including the motor cortex, cerebellum, and basal ganglia, are actively involved. If we were truly using only 10 percent of our brain, it would be difficult to coordinate our movements and perform tasks requiring fine motor control, such as playing a musical instrument or typing.

Brain Damage: In cases of brain damage or injury to specific regions, individuals often experience impairments related to the affected area. For example, damage to the frontal lobe can result in changes in personality, decision-making, and impulse control. If only 10 percent of the brain were in use, such localized injuries would have minimal impact on overall functioning.

The "Ten percent of the brain" myth is an inaccurate portrayal of human brain functioning. Our brains are highly active and engaged in various tasks and processes, utilizing different regions for different functions. The myth likely originated from a misinterpretation of neurological research, and it has been debunked by scientific evidence and studies on brain activity.

Why and How?

Picture this: the legend of the all-mighty brain, capable of mind-blowing miracles that put even the most dazzling magic tricks to shame. It's like having a superhero in your noggin, right? Well, not so fast, my friend! Let's dive into the mythical realm of limitless mental powers, but don't forget your grains of salt.

First off, our brains may be incredible organs, but they come with their own rulebook. Think of it as an IKEA instruction manual - there are limits and guidelines to follow. Sure, you can build some impressive furniture, but you won't be constructing an entire skyscraper from those flat-packed Swedish goodies.

Imagine if we could manipulate reality with our minds. Want a pizza? Boom! It appears before you. But hold your toppings, because the laws of physics crash the party. No matter how hard you focus,

your mind can't simply bend spoons or make objects float like a lazy magician. Gravity is not a big fan of your mental shenanigans.

Here are a few reasons why the myth of unlimited power of the mind is not supported by scientific evidence:

Biological Constraints: The human brain, which is the physical foundation of the mind, operates within certain physiological boundaries. It has a specific structure and functioning that impose limits on cognitive processes, memory capacity, and sensory perception.

Physical Limitations: The mind's influence over the physical world is limited by the laws of nature. While thoughts and intentions can motivate action and behavior, they cannot defy the fundamental principles of physics or alter reality at will.

Cognitive Abilities: While the mind can learn, adapt, and develop various mental skills, there are inherent limitations to human cognition. For example, the brain has finite processing capacity, attentional limits, and constraints on memory recall, which affect our ability to process vast amounts of information simultaneously or perform complex tasks effortlessly.

Emotional and Psychological Factors: Human emotions, biases, and subjective experiences can influence how we perceive and interpret the world. They can create cognitive biases, such as confirmation bias or cognitive dissonance, which can distort our thinking and limit our ability to reason objectively.

Ethical Considerations: Even if the mind had unlimited power, ethical concerns arise when discussing the potential consequences of such abilities. The misuse or abuse of unlimited mental power could lead to ethical dilemmas, manipulation, and harm to oneself or others.

Scientists believe that the human brain has a storage capacity of about 2.5 million gigabytes, which is a lot! However, it's important to understand that having such a large capacity doesn't mean we can become supernatural or have extraordinary abilities. Contrary to the popular myth, we actually use all parts of our brain, even though we might not be aware of it. We are still human beings, with our own limitations and capabilities. So while our brains are amazing and can hold an incredible amount of information, it doesn't make us superhuman. We should appreciate and embrace our human nature while exploring the potential of our remarkable brains

It's important to approach claims about the unlimited power of the mind with skepticism and critical thinking, relying on scientific evidence and rational inquiry to understand the true capabilities of human cognition. While the human mind is undoubtedly extraordinary, it operates within certain boundaries and is subject to the limitations of our biology, physical reality, and cognitive processes.

In the vast tapestry of human existence, there are those who perceive themselves as less capable, as if destiny had dealt them a hand bereft of brilliance and potential. Yet, when the stage is set and the curtain rises, these seemingly unremarkable souls often astonish the world with their resplendent achievements. Success, it seems, is not merely a consequence of innate talents or predetermined aptitude, but a symphony woven together by the interplay of numerous harmonious factors.

The journey towards triumph is paved with unyielding perseverance, an unwavering commitment to continual effort. Those who believe in their supposed limitations may succumb to the temptation of complacency, held captive by their self-imposed boundaries. But those who rise above such self-doubt, driven by an insatiable thirst for progress, embrace the arduous path of continuous improvement. With every step forward, they refine their skills, honing their abilities until they become instruments of unfathomable proficiency.

However, the quest for success is not a solitary pursuit, for the choice of fields plays a crucial role in the orchestration of triumph. Each individual possesses a unique palette of passions, a kaleidoscope of interests waiting to be explored. By heeding the whispers of their hearts and finding solace in the realms that ignite their souls, those who perceive themselves as less capable can discover hidden wellsprings of talent and brilliance. The alchemy of success lies in the alignment of one's pursuits with their intrinsic inclinations, allowing the fires of passion to kindle the way to greatness.

Yet, amidst the labyrinthine paths of self-discovery and tireless exertion, a beacon of guidance can illuminate the way at the most opportune moments. The timely intervention of mentors, teachers, or guides who recognize the untapped potential within these seemingly unremarkable individuals can forge a transformative trajectory. Like a compass pointing true north, these wise custodians offer insights, nurture dreams, and instill belief, guiding those who are inclined to doubt their own capabilities towards the realization of their extraordinary potential.

To illustrate this intricate tapestry of success, let us journey to a humble village nestled in the emerald valleys, where a young lad named Aiden resides. Aiden, convinced of his own inadequacy, finds solace in the shadows, doubting his capacity to make a difference. However, through a fortuitous encounter with a wise elder, he discovers the art of storytelling—a craft that allows him to weave his thoughts into words, captivating hearts and minds. Encouraged by his mentor's unwavering belief in his storytelling prowess, Aiden embarks on a journey of self-improvement. He tirelessly hones his linguistic skills, studying the masters and experimenting with various narrative styles. As the years pass, Aiden's once-muted voice resonates across continents, enchanting audiences with tales of wonder and inspiration.

In this enchanting tale, we witness the transformative power that arises when continuous effort, the pursuit of one's true calling, and the guidance of a mentor converge. The young lad, who once believed himself to be less capable, shatters the shackles of self-doubt to carve a remarkable path to success.

So, let it be known that success is not an elusive mirage, attainable only by the fortunate few endowed with innate brilliance. Instead, it emerges as a result of the symphony conducted by relentless effort, the embrace of one's passions, the acquisition of knowledge, and the timely guidance that kindles the spark of potential. In the grand tapestry of life, those who believe themselves to be less capable possess within them the seeds of greatness, awaiting only the nurturing touch of belief, perseverance, and the guidance that can transform their perceived limitations into soaring achievements

CHAPTER 3

Multitasking star? Nope, You are not.

"Every single time we switch there is a cost. It's draining. It's taking longer to do the same thing."

—DR. SAHAR YOUSEF, COGNITIVE NEUROSCIENTIST, UC BERKELEY

Imagine you're in a restaurant with only one staff member. He take your order, go to the kitchen to cook the food, bring it to your table, and then collect the payment. Now, let's think about this staff member's tasks. Even though it may seem like He is doing multiple things at once, He is actually not multitasking.

In a similar way, your brain works like this staff member. It can't truly multitask. Instead, it switches quickly between different tasks, a process called context-shifting. Each time you switch tasks, there is a brief moment where your brain needs to refocus and adjust to the new task. This transition takes time and can lead to mistakes or errors. Moreover, the act of switching tasks itself takes time. So, even though you may think you're saving time by multitasking, it actually takes longer to complete both tasks compared to if you focused on them one at a time. For example, if you dedicated your full attention to writing the email first and then made the phone call, you would likely finish both tasks more quickly and with better accuracy.

According to the book "Brain Rules," research has shown that when people try to multitask, their error rate increases by 50%, and it takes them twice as long to complete tasks compared to focusing on one thing at a time.

When your brain focuses on a single task, a part of the brain called the prefrontal cortex plays a crucial role. The front part of this region sets the goal or intention, like wanting a cookie, and the back part communicates with the rest of the brain, helping you reach for the cookie jar and confirming whether you have the cookie or not.

The impact of multitasking is expected to be mostly limited to the short term, although comprehensive studies to fully address this question are currently lacking. One study, based on correlation, revealed that individuals who engage in high levels of media multitasking tend to have smaller brain volumes in a specific region called the cingulate cortex, which plays a crucial role in regulating emotions and behavior. Nevertheless, it remains uncertain whether multitasking directly causes permanent alterations in the brain or if individuals with smaller volumes in this brain region are inherently predisposed to multitasking tendencies.

While the available evidence suggests that multitasking may have transient effects, it is important to note the absence of definitive research that can establish a conclusive link. The aforementioned correlational study offers insights into the potential relationship between multitasking and brain structure, specifically highlighting the association between high media multitasking and reduced volume in the cingulate cortex.

This brain region is essential for emotional and behavioral regulation, indicating a possible impact of multitasking on cognitive processes.

However, the exact nature of this relationship remains uncertain. It is plausible that extensive multitasking leads to structural changes in the brain, resulting in smaller volumes in the cingulate cortex. Conversely, it is also possible that individuals with naturally smaller volumes in this region are more prone to engaging in multitasking behaviors. Without further research, it is challenging to determine causation definitively.

To gain a comprehensive understanding of the long-term effects of multitasking on the brain, additional studies are necessary. These studies should employ rigorous methodologies, such as longitudinal research designs that track individuals over an extended period.

By examining brain structure and function before and after engaging in multitasking activities, researchers can begin to unravel the intricate relationship between multitasking and its potential impacts on the brain.

In summary, while the existing evidence indicates a potential association between multitasking and reduced brain volume in the cingulate cortex, further investigations are required to establish a definitive link and determine whether the effects of multitasking on the brain are temporary or permanent.

You may believe that multitasking comes naturally to you and that you excel at it. However, you're not alone in thinking this way. In fact, a survey revealed that 93% of individuals believe they can multitask better than or at least as well as the average person. Unfortunately, multitasking has its downsides, one of which is its negative impact on metacognition.

Metacognition refers to our ability to monitor and evaluate our own performance on a task. When we engage in multitasking, it appears to impair this metacognitive ability. In other words, we become less aware of how well we are actually performing on the tasks we're juggling. This creates a deceptive situation where we may believe we are doing just fine, even though our performance is actually being compromised.

This lack of awareness can be particularly risky in certain situations, such as driving while texting. When we engage in this type of multitasking, our performance behind the wheel is likely to suffer, yet we may mistakenly perceive ourselves as being capable of handling both activities simultaneously.

Despite the common belief that we are skilled multitaskers, research indicates that multitasking hampers our metacognitive abilities and can lead to reduced performance. It is crucial to recognize these risks, especially in situations where multitasking can pose a threat to our safety and the safety of others.

Prioritize your tasks

Sometimes, we tend to multitask because everything appears equally important. For instance, you might be working on a simple task like creating a LinkedIn post or designing an image when suddenly another request comes in. In such situations, we often feel compelled to switch gears and tackle the new request right away.

To manage multitasking effectively, it's crucial to understand the relative importance and impact of each task. This way, when a new request arrives but is less significant than what you're currently working on, you can resist the temptation to multitask and stay focused on your ongoing task. On the other hand, if a new request is more important than your current task, you can shift your attention to the new request and temporarily set aside what you were previously doing.

Being busy doesn't mean you are being productive.

A study from the University of Utah showed that people who claimed to be good at multitasking actually struggled when they had to remember things and solve math problems at the same time. The best performers in the study were the ones who rarely multitasked in their daily lives.

We don't know for sure if multitasking causes a decline in attention and an increase in distractions, or if people who are easily distracted are more likely to multitask. However, there are some characteristics that are common among frequent multitaskers. They tend to be impulsive and enjoy seeking new and intense experiences. It's possible that people with shorter attention spans are naturally drawn to multitasking.

Regardless of the cause, the problem of multitasking is likely to get worse as we have more and more media options available to us. The more people give in to the temptation to multitask, the more it will affect their ability to focus on challenging tasks.

A study conducted by the Institute of Psychiatry at the University of London examined 1100 employees from a British company. The researchers discovered that engaging in multitasking with electronic media can lead to a temporary decline in IQ, with a reduction of up to 15 points. Surprisingly, this decrease in IQ is even greater than the impact of skipping a night's sleep or using Marijuana. As a result, most adults who engage in multitasking with electronic media experience a drop in IQ comparable to that of an 8-year-old child.

These findings are particularly relevant for today's teenagers who often believe they can simultaneously watch videos, listen to music, and text their friends while doing homework. However, extensive research now confirms that this approach is ineffective for learning or completing tasks efficiently.

Lastly, it is important to remember that multitasking does not make you smarter.

Stress, the silent Killer

Numerous studies have revealed that individuals who frequently engage in multitasking experience elevated levels of the stress hormone cortisol. While cortisol is beneficial in moderate amounts, excessive levels can lead to a range of negative effects on the body. These effects include reproductive problems, heightened inflammation, elevated blood sugar levels, weakened immune system, increased accumulation of belly fat, and damage to the brain regions responsible for memory function.

Furthermore, multitaskers often encounter challenges related to working memory, which impairs their ability to make sound and rational decisions. Working memory refers to the capacity to temporarily hold and manipulate information in mind for cognitive tasks. When this cognitive function is compromised, individuals may find it harder to focus, organize their thoughts, and effectively process information.

For instance, imagine a student who is simultaneously texting, browsing social media, and studying for an exam. The constant switching between tasks and distractions may lead to heightened stress levels, an impaired ability to retain information, and difficulty in making logical connections during the exam. Similarly, a professional juggling multiple projects, emails, and phone calls might experience increased stress, reduced efficiency, and decreased problem-solving skills.

In summary, multitasking not only triggers an increase in cortisol levels, causing various detrimental effects on the body, but it also hampers working memory, impacting one's cognitive abilities and decision-making skills. It is crucial to recognize the potential consequences of chronic multitasking and prioritize focused, single-tasking approaches to optimize both mental well-being and productivity.

Pomorodo Technique

The Pomodoro Technique is a time management method designed to help individuals improve focus, productivity, and manage multitasking effectively. It involves breaking your work into intervals, typically 25 minutes in length, called "Pomodoros." Here's a simple explanation of how the technique works:

Choose a Task: Select the task you want to work on. It could be studying, writing, coding, or any other activity that requires your attention.

Set a Timer: Set a timer for 25 minutes, which represents one Pomodoro. You can use a physical timer, a timer app on your phone, or even a website that offers Pomodoro timers.

Work with Focus: Start working on your chosen task with complete focus and concentration. Avoid any distractions or interruptions during this Pomodoro. Try to give your best effort and make progress on the task at hand.

Take a Short Break: Once the 25 minutes are up, take a short break of around 5 minutes. Use this time to relax, stretch, or do something unrelated to work. It helps you recharge and prepares you for the next Pomodoro.

Repeat and Track: Repeat the cycle by setting the timer for another 25 minutes and continuing to work on your task. After completing four Pomodoros, take a longer break of around 15-30 minutes. This break allows you to rejuvenate and maintain productivity throughout the day.

Manage Multitasking: If you have multiple tasks to tackle, prioritize them and allocate specific Pomodoros to each task. For example, you can work on Task A for one Pomodoro, then switch to Task B for the next Pomodoro, and so on. This approach helps prevent burnout and ensures progress on various tasks.

Adjust as Needed: The Pomodoro Technique is flexible, so you can adjust the time intervals based on your preferences and the nature of your work. If 25 minutes feels too short or too long, you can experiment with different durations until you find what works best for you.

Remember, the key to the Pomodoro Technique is maintaining focus during each Pomodoro and using breaks strategically to rest and recharge. By managing your time effectively and working in dedicated intervals, you can enhance your productivity and manage multitasking more efficiently.

CHAPTER 4

Reality or Negativity

And the longer you ignore it, the bigger it gets! It's like that old saying, "A problem ignored is a problem doubled."

Oh no, I'm not here to destroy anyone's positive thinking! In fact, I'm all for it! But let's be real, sometimes you can't just positive-think your way out of a bad situation.

But you're right, sometimes people use motivation or positive thinking as a way to avoid facing difficult realities. It's like trying to run away from a tiger in your bedroom by pretending you're a little kitty cat who can take on a tiger. Sure, it's cute and funny to imagine, but it's not going to solve the problem at hand!

So, if there's a tiger in your bedroom and you don't have the strength to face it, what can you do? Well, you could try calling for help, or finding a way to escape the room safely. You could also try to stay calm and avoid making sudden movements that might provoke the tiger.

Escaping and avoiding undesirable realities is not a recent phenomenon; it has been present throughout human history. At its core, escapism serves as a mechanism to avoid confronting uncomfortable aspects of oneself, personal beliefs, or the harsh realities that may cause distress. Understanding the psychology behind escapism requires acknowledging an important factor: the desire to escape can arise as a reaction to external stimuli such as stress, danger, or adversity. However, it can also be a strategic response for emotional survival.

Escapism serves as a coping mechanism in response to challenging circumstances or overwhelming emotions. It offers a temporary respite from the burdens of reality, allowing individuals to find solace, recharge, and regain their emotional equilibrium. By seeking moments of escape, individuals can distance themselves from the immediate troubles they face, granting them a much-needed break and relief from the pressures of everyday life.

Since the dawn of human cognitive evolution, humans have had a natural inclination to create imaginary worlds within their minds and immerse themselves in them. This innate tendency has persisted throughout history. In the late 2003, during the early stages of information technology's development, Philip Rosedale introduced a revolutionary web platform called Second Life. This platform offered users the opportunity to construct and inhabit a virtual representation of themselves, essentially living a parallel life within a perfect digital world.

As time went on, numerous similar games and platforms emerged, providing individuals with additional avenues to escape into their own imaginative realms. The underlying idea behind this phenomenon is that humans possess an inherent instinct to detach themselves from the realities of consciousness. Engaging in these virtual worlds serves as one of many tools used by individuals to satisfy their need for motivation and fulfillment.

Consider it as a means of finding solace or seeking new experiences. It allows individuals to explore possibilities and realities beyond what is physically attainable or present in their everyday lives. These virtual spaces provide an outlet for creativity, social interaction, and personal expression. People may find joy in building and designing virtual environments, creating avatars that represent their ideal selves, or connecting with others who share their interests and passions.

The natural instinct of humans to detach themselves from the awareness of reality is just one of the many tools they employ for motivation.

Human beings possess an innate tendency to seek avenues that allow them to escape from the immediate constraints of reality. This inclination is rooted in the desire for motivation and inspiration. Creating and immersing oneself in alternative worlds or engaging with imaginative experiences can serve as a means of motivation for individuals.

By distancing themselves from the consciousness of everyday reality, humans can tap into their creativity, explore new possibilities, and find renewed motivation. These ventures into imaginative realms can fuel their passion, drive, and desire to pursue goals and aspirations.

However, it is important to note that this instinctual detachment from reality should not be seen as the sole tool for motivation. Humans utilize a wide range of methods and strategies to fuel their motivation, including seeking personal connections, setting goals, pursuing interests, engaging in physical activities, and embracing challenges.

Ultimately, the instinct to distance oneself from reality is just one aspect of the complex and multifaceted nature of human motivation. It is essential to recognize the importance of maintaining a balanced approach, integrating both the exploration of imaginative realms and active participation in the real world, in order to cultivate holistic motivation and a fulfilling life.

Ask for Help

In seeking aid, we find strength's embrace,
Through humble request, we quicken our pace.
For in the arms of assistance, we rise,
Unlocking potential, reaching new skies.

Another risk associated with having an inflated sense of self-esteem is our hesitance to accept assistance. The illusion we construct around ourselves can deceive us into thinking that seeking help is a negative thing. However, it is important to recognize that accepting help from others can often lead us to overcome various obstacles more smoothly and reach significant milestones.

Imagine a student who believes they are extremely intelligent and capable of excelling in all academic subjects without any support. Due to their inflated self-esteem, they may resist seeking help from teachers or classmates when they encounter difficulties in understanding certain concepts. As a result, they may struggle to grasp the material, fall behind in their studies, and potentially miss out on important learning opportunities.

On the other hand, if the student acknowledges their limitations and accepts assistance, they can benefit greatly. By seeking guidance from teachers or collaborating with peers, they can clarify their doubts, gain deeper insights, and improve their overall understanding of the subject matter. This, in turn, can lead them to achieve better academic performance and successfully reach important educational milestones.

The danger of having inflated self-esteem lies in our tendency to reject help due to the illusion of self-sufficiency. However, it is crucial to understand that accepting assistance from others can be highly beneficial. By embracing support when needed, we can overcome challenges more effectively, reach significant milestones, and ultimately grow and develop as individuals.

Moreover, embracing both the act of accepting help and extending help to others can contribute to the strengthening of our social fabric. By recognizing the importance of our social responsibilities, we not only enhance our own lives but also pave the way for a more pleasant and sustainable living environment for future generations. It is essential to acknowledge that our duty extends beyond our present existence and encompasses the creation of favorable conditions for the well-being of those who will follow.

Consider the concept of community engagement and support. When individuals come together, offer assistance, and collaborate towards common goals, they foster a sense of unity and cohesion within the society they inhabit. This collective effort not only improves the lives of individuals in the present but also sets the foundation for a more vibrant and harmonious community in the future.

Let's imagine a neighborhood where residents actively participate in initiatives aimed at improving the local environment. They organize clean-up drives, establish community gardens, and support educational programs for children. Through these joint efforts, they create a safe, clean, and nurturing environment for their own families and for the upcoming generations. By recognizing their social duty and taking proactive steps, they contribute to a better quality of life for both themselves and the future residents of their neighborhood.

Embracing the acts of accepting and providing help goes beyond personal gratification. It plays a crucial role in strengthening the social fabric of our communities. By fulfilling our social responsibilities and actively working towards creating favorable conditions for future generations, we foster a more enjoyable and sustainable living situation for all.

Motivation is a fickle thing. It can give you a burst of energy and focus, but it often doesn't last.

For example, you might listen to a motivational speech or have a conversation with a friend that inspires you to work towards your goals. You might feel energized and focused for the rest of the day, but the next day you might wake up feeling tired and unmotivated.

This is because motivation is a fleeting emotion. It comes and goes, and it's not always reliable.

What you need is consistency.

Consistency is the key to achieving your goals. It's about taking action, even when you don't feel motivated. It's about showing up every day, even when you don't feel like it.

When you're consistent, you build momentum. You start to see results, and that gives you more motivation to keep going.

So how do you become more consistent?

Here are a few tips:

- Set small, achievable goals.
- Break down your goals into smaller steps.
- Reward yourself for your progress.
- Find a support system.
- Consistency is not easy, but it's worth it.

Achieving consistency may not come effortlessly, but the rewards it brings are truly worthwhile. With unwavering consistency, you have the power to accomplish anything you envision.

Here's an analogy to help you understand the importance of consistency:

Imagine you're trying to build a sandcastle. If you just build it once, it will probably be washed away by the next wave. But if you keep building it, day after day, eventually you'll have a sandcastle that's strong enough to withstand the waves.

The same is true with motivation. If you just rely on motivation, it will eventually fade away. But if you're consistent, you'll eventually achieve your goals.

So don't give up on your dreams.

Be consistent, and you'll see results.

CHAPTER 5

You're one of a kind, But you're not an Alien

Oh boy, you're the Jesus, huh? That's quite a claim! I mean, sure, you can do so many activities at once that it's like you've got an octopus for a brain! And your ideas? They're flowing faster than a chocolate fountain at a dessert buffet, creating a flurry of creativity that's out of this world!

But hey, let's keep it real for a moment. Having an inflated sense of self-esteem and thinking you're the second coming of Jesus might be a sign that you've taken a detour on the way to normal town and ended up in euphoricville. And trust me, that's not where you want to be setting up your homestead.

Remember, you don't need to be a Superman or a Wonder Woman to achieve your goals. We're all just regular humans trying to figure out this crazy thing called life. Goals are something you discover as you go along, like finding a hidden treasure chest in a video game or stumbling upon a sale at your favorite store. They're not something you're born with, like a belly button or an urge to dance when your jam comes on.

So, let's tone down the Jesus talk a bit and embrace the awesomeness of being a flawed, but fabulous, human being. You'll find that life's adventures are much more enjoyable when you're not trying to walk on water or turn water into wine. Cheers to being uniquely you, without all the heavenly bells and whistles! Amen to that! Or, you know, whatever floats your boat. Just remember to keep it funny, folks!

Social Rules and impact

The issue of social rules is further compounded by their often rigid and inflexible nature. These rules, which have developed over time, can become monolithic, meaning they are fixed and unchanging, without room for variation or individuality. This can restrict the natural diversity that exists within humanity, and confine individuals to conform to societal expectations.

For example, in some cultures, there may be strict norms regarding gender roles, where men are expected to be assertive and dominant, while women are expected to be passive and nurturing. This monolithic social rule can limit individuals who do not fit into these traditional gender roles, such as a man who prefers to be nurturing and empathetic, or a woman who aspires to be assertive and ambitious. Such individuals may feel constrained by these rigid social norms, which can stifle their personal growth and self-expression.

Similarly, social rules can also dictate what is considered acceptable in terms of appearance, lifestyle, or beliefs. For instance, a person who deviates from the conventional beauty standards of their society may face criticism or ostracism, which can lead to low self-esteem and a sense of not belonging. Likewise, someone who holds unconventional or minority beliefs may face discrimination or marginalization, which can inhibit their freedom of expression and intellectual exploration.

In some cases, the pressure to conform to social rules can cause individuals to suppress their true selves and adopt a facade to fit in with societal expectations. For instance, a person may hide their sexual orientation, religious beliefs, or cultural heritage in order to avoid social repercussions or discrimination. This can lead to a sense of internal conflict and emotional distress, as individuals struggle to reconcile their authentic identity with the pressures of conformity.

In conclusion, the monolithic nature of social rules can be problematic as it can stifle the natural diversity that exists within humanity. It can restrict individuals from expressing their unique identities and conforming to societal expectations can sometimes lead to internal conflict and emotional distress. It is important to recognize and respect the differences among individuals, and understand that being different does not make one better or worse. Embracing diversity and promoting inclusivity can foster a more open, accepting, and inclusive society where individuals are free to express their authentic selves without fear of judgment or discrimination.

While each person is inherently unique, it's important to acknowledge that we are also part of a larger social context. We may have our own distinct qualities, experiences, and perspectives, but we are not completely isolated beings.

While you are indeed unique, you are not an alien from another planet. You are a part of the human society, bound by its social norms and rules.

Although you possess your own individuality, you can still find commonalities with others. Despite our differences, we often share similar emotions, desires, and struggles, which can create connections and foster empathy among individuals.

Remember, being unique does not mean being completely detached from society or others. It's about celebrating our individuality while also recognizing our shared humanity. Embracing both our uniqueness and our commonalities can lead to a more inclusive and compassionate perspective towards ourselves and others.

Conditioning, the master manipulator

Conditioning plays a significant role in how we respond to the world around us. It's like how our brains are wired to react to certain stimuli based on our desires and aspirations. For example, let's say you've always dreamt of becoming a professional athlete, and you've been working hard to achieve that goal. One day, a well-respected coach tells you that you have unlimited potential and can achieve anything you set your mind to. You start to internalize this message and believe it because it aligns with your dreams and hopes. However, as a result, you may start neglecting your other talents or abilities because you're solely focused on pursuing a career in sports.

Imagine you're at a party, and there's a plate of freshly baked cookies sitting on the table. Your eyes widen, your mouth waters, and that heavenly smell fills your nostrils. You're practically drooling! Then, your friend walks over and says, "Hey, those cookies are terrible for you. They'll make you gain a ton of weight!" Suddenly, your enthusiasm fizzles out like a deflated balloon, and you walk away from the cookies with a heavy heart.

This is how conditioning can influence our behavior and perception of ourselves. We're inclined to accept messages or actions that resonate with our desires and hopes, especially if they come from trusted sources. But the danger is that we may forget our other capabilities or strengths because we're so fixated on one particular path. It's like wearing blinders that limit our perspective and hinder us from exploring our full potential.

The key is to be aware of the influence of conditioning and take a step back to critically evaluate the messages we receive. We need to consider our own abilities, talents, and aspirations holistically, rather than solely focusing on one narrow view. By being mindful and open-minded, we can avoid getting trapped in limiting beliefs or expectations and embrace our diverse capabilities. So, let's keep our eyes and ears open, stay true to ourselves, and not let conditioning box us in!

Embracing Realistic Paths to Success

imagine you're a penguin who dreams of flying high in the sky like an eagle. You're determined and passionate about it, but there's just one tiny problem - you have wings that are designed for swimming, not flying. Despite this limitation, you're determined to go on with your goal and start building a makeshift airplane using fish as fuel. You strap on your fish-powered wings and take off into the air, only to realize that you're not soaring gracefully like an eagle, but instead flapping around awkwardly, crashing into trees, and scaring off other birds with your fishy smell.

Or let's say you're a cat who dreams of becoming a renowned chef. You're eager to explore the world of culinary arts, but there's just one problem - you have paws instead of hands, and you can't handle a knife or flip a pancake to save your life. Undeterred, you don an apron and start attempting to cook with your paws, resulting in a chaotic kitchen with pots and pans flying everywhere, food burnt to a crisp, and a very confused and hungry family staring at you in disbelief.

Acknowledge your limitations and finding practical ways to work around them. While it's essential to dream big and pursue our goals, blindly ignoring our limitations can lead to comical and often disastrous outcomes. It's like trying to fit a square peg into a round hole, or like wearing shoes that are two sizes too small - uncomfortable and impractical.

Instead, we can embrace our limitations and find creative ways to overcome them. We can leverage our strengths, seek help from others, and adapt our approach to achieve our goals in a more realistic and practical manner. It's about being resourceful, flexible, and willing to learn from our mistakes with a sense of humor. After all, life is too short to take ourselves too seriously, and sometimes the best adventures come from embracing our quirks and limitations along the way. So, let's laugh, learn, and make the most of our unique journeys, limitations and all!

We are designed to fail

"Fall seven times and stand up eight." - Japanese Proverb

- I am not good enough
- I should give up
- I should never have tried
- I was always going to fail
- I will never survive this
- I am being irresponsible

It appears that these thoughts linger in the minds of many, particularly in moments tainted by the scent of failure. It's natural to feel this way, and there's no need to fret or question. The reality is that instead of triumphing over failure, we often find ourselves succumbing to its grip.

In life, we all experience failure. It can be painful, and it often leaves us feeling helpless. However, failure is not the end; it is merely a stepping stone on our journey to success.

Think about the countless studies conducted on failure. They highlight the transformative power it has on individuals. I want to discuss on the natural process of failure, acknowledging that it is an inherent part of our lives. Rather than providing you with mere mantras to overcome failure, it aims to illuminate the opportunities that arise from this process.

Failure, you see, is not a final verdict. It is a chance to begin again, armed with newfound wisdom and intelligence. As Henry Ford wisely said, "Failure is only the opportunity to begin again, this time more intelligently."

So, let us embark on this exploration together. Let us embrace the falls, learn from them, and rise even stronger. I will try to guide you through the hidden gifts that failure offers, helping you navigate through the challenges and ultimately lead you towards a brighter, more fulfilling path.

Remember, every time you fall, summon the strength to stand up again. Embrace failure as a teacher, and let it empower you to take your next steps with greater wisdom and resilience.

Failure is an opportunity

Failure is not always a bad thing. In fact, it can be a valuable learning experience and realise you are half way to winning.

Failure can be broken down into two distinct parts: the emotional aspect and the realization aspect. Everyone experiences the emotional part of failure in a similar manner. It is common to feel a sense of depression, worthlessness, and desperation. These emotions vary depending on the individual's past experiences in dealing with failures. However, it is important not to dwell too long on these emotional setbacks. Instead, it is crucial to let go and move forward.

The second part of failure, the realization aspect, holds great significance. It is here that we must confront the reality of the situation. To truly understand and learn from our failures, we must be able to assess and measure them. But how does one measure failure? It is through gaining experience and evaluating our journey towards achieving our goals that we can gauge the extent of our failure.

For example, imagine failing a job interview on your first attempt and not progressing to the second round. Despite the disappointment, this failure grants you valuable experience. It allows you to reflect upon the interview process, identify areas where improvements are needed, and recognize the gaps that prevented you from securing the job. These insights can only be gained if you are willing to acknowledge and learn from your failure. It is at this point of realization that opportunities for growth and development emerge.

Some individuals may choose to deny or reject their failures, adopting a short-term approach. However, this denial hinders personal growth in the long run. By embracing failure, understanding its lessons, and seeking opportunities for improvement, we can embark on a path of continuous growth and eventual success. Remember, failure is not an endpoint but a stepping stone towards greater achievements.

Failure has a significant influence on our social psychology. One of the reasons why we tend to cling onto our failures is because we worry about how others will perceive us. We become consumed with thoughts about how our potential failures might impact the image we want to maintain, and over time, this can develop into a fear of failure, which sometimes even becomes a full-blown phobia.

The underlying message conveyed throughout this book revolves around the concept of facing reality. Fear of failure stands as one of the main obstacles that obstruct our path to success. But how does this fear manifest?

One common scenario is lacking the confidence to undertake a task, leading us to avoid attempting it altogether. It's essential to remember that in certain instances, the task may genuinely be beyond our abilities.

Another factor contributing to the fear of failure is the pressure to meet other people's expectations. However, it's important to note that it's not our responsibility to live up to the expectations others have of us.

Let's consider the example of Sarah, a talented painter who dreams of showcasing her artwork in a prestigious gallery. However, Sarah has always been apprehensive about failure and how others might perceive her if her artwork is not well-received.

Due to this fear, Sarah hesitates to submit her paintings to the gallery for consideration. She worries about the possibility of rejection and imagines how it might impact her reputation as an artist. This fear gradually grows, and she becomes reluctant to take the necessary steps to pursue her dream.

Sarah's fear of failure has created a psychological barrier that prevents her from taking action. She lacks confidence in her abilities and doubts whether her artwork will meet the gallery's expectations. As a result, she finds herself stuck in a state of inaction, unwilling to take the risk and face potential failure.

In this example, Sarah's fear of failure is fueled by concerns about social judgment and meeting external expectations. This fear holds her back from fully embracing her artistic passion and limits her opportunities for growth and recognition.

By understanding the influence of social psychology on our fear of failure, we can begin to address and overcome these barriers. Through self-reflection, building confidence, and shifting our focus from external validation to personal growth, we can empower ourselves to confront failure and pursue our goals with greater resilience and determination.

Numerous thoughts can trigger the fear of failure, each one playing a role in shaping our mindset and affecting our willingness to take risks and pursue our goals.

How to replan a failure?

Identify, Realise, Rewind, Try again and Repeat ! So simple as this.

---

1. **a) Identify and Realise the failure.** What went wrong? What were the root causes of the failure? This may involve some introspection, talking to others who were involved, or reviewing data.

Let's consider a personal example of a failure in achieving a fitness goal: running a marathon.

The failure: Despite setting a goal to complete a marathon, I was unable to finish the race within the desired time frame and fell short of my expectations.

Step 1: Identifying the failure To acknowledge the failure, I need to recognize that I did not achieve my goal of completing the marathon within the targeted time.

Step 2: Examining what went wrong To understand the failure, I can analyze various factors that may have contributed to the outcome:

Insufficient training: I may not have followed a well-structured training plan, leading to inadequate physical conditioning and endurance for the marathon distance.

Ineffective pacing strategy: I might have started the race too fast or misjudged my energy expenditure throughout the course, resulting in exhaustion or muscle fatigue.

Nutrition and hydration: Poor fueling strategies or inadequate hydration during training and on race day could have impacted my performance and hindered my ability to sustain energy levels.

Step 3: Identifying root causes To uncover the root causes, I can engage in introspection, seek input from others involved, and review relevant data:

Self-reflection: I can reflect on my commitment level, discipline, and consistency during training. Did I prioritize my workouts and adhere to the training plan effectively? Did I push myself enough during training runs?

Feedback from others: Conversations with running coaches, fellow runners, or training partners who observed my progress or participated in the race can provide insights into areas for improvement. They may highlight specific issues with my training approach, pacing, or nutritional choices.

Data analysis: Reviewing training logs, race splits, and heart rate data (if available) can provide quantitative information to identify patterns and potential factors contributing to the failure. This could include analyzing training mileage, average pace, or identifying critical points in the race where performance declined.

By exploring the failure, identifying the factors that went wrong, and understanding the root causes, I can learn valuable lessons for future endeavors. This process of introspection, seeking feedback from others, and reviewing relevant data empowers me to make informed adjustments in my training approach, pacing strategy, or nutrition plan. It enables personal growth and increases the chances of achieving success in future fitness goals.

1. **b) Rewind.** This means going back to the beginning and reviewing your plan. What could you have done differently to avoid the failure? What changes need to be made to your plan?

In the context of the marathon example, let's say you failed to achieve your desired time or performance in the race. When you rewind and review your plan, there are several aspects you could consider to identify what could have been done differently and what changes need to be made:

Training: Evaluate your training regimen leading up to the marathon. Did you have a structured and consistent training plan? Consider factors such as the volume, intensity, and specificity of your training sessions. Perhaps you could have increased your mileage gradually, incorporated more speed work, or focused on specific aspects of endurance and strength.

Nutrition: Analyze your nutrition and hydration strategy during training and the race itself. Did you fuel your body adequately before, during, and after workouts? Did you consume enough carbohydrates to sustain your energy levels? Reflect on whether you could have made better choices regarding your pre-race meals and race fueling strategy.

Rest and Recovery: Examine your rest and recovery practices. Did you allow enough time for rest and proper sleep between training sessions? Did you incorporate active recovery activities such as stretching, foam rolling, or massage? Consider whether you could have prioritized recovery more effectively to avoid fatigue and overtraining.

Mental Preparation: Reflect on your mental preparation for the marathon. Did you have a positive mindset and a strong mental game? Consider whether you could have employed techniques such as visualization, goal setting, or mindfulness to enhance your mental focus and resilience during the race.

Race Strategy: Evaluate your race strategy. Did you have a well-defined plan for pacing and managing your effort throughout the marathon?

Consider whether you started too fast, didn't pace yourself properly, or encountered unexpected challenges during the race. Analyze your decision-making during the race and identify areas where you could have made more informed choices.

1. **c)** Try again. This is the most important step. Once you have identified the root causes of the failure and made changes to your plan, you need to try again. Don't give up on your goals just because you failed once.

1. d) Repeat. The process of identifying, realizing, rewinding, trying again, and repeating is an iterative process. You may need to go through these steps multiple times before you succeed.

Failure is an experience.

Failure is a part of life. Everyone experiences failure at some point. When we fail, we can learn what went wrong and how we can do better next time. We can also develop resilience and determination, which are essential qualities for success.

Experience is not good or bad, every experience is a stepping stone on the way forward. Every experience, whether positive or negative, can teach us something. Even failures can be valuable experiences. They can teach us what we don't want to do, and they can help us to develop the skills and knowledge we need to succeed.

As far as life is concerned, avoidable future tragedies will also lead to success. These failures will help you with that. The statement "avoidable future tragedies" refers to the things that we can learn from our failures so that we can avoid making the same mistakes in the future. For example, if we fail a test, we can learn from our mistakes and study harder for the next test. If we fail a job interview, we can learn from our mistakes and practice our interviewing skills.

By learning from our failures, we can avoid making the same mistakes in the future. This will help us to succeed in the long run.

Let's say that you are trying to start your own business. You work hard and put in a lot of effort, but your business fails. This is a failure, but it is also an experience. You can learn from your mistakes and try again. You can also develop the skills and knowledge you need to succeed in the future.

The next time you start a business, you will be more prepared. You will know what to do and what not to do. You will also be more confident in your abilities. This is because you have the experience of failure to guide you.

CHAPTER 7

Defining Success - Personal Note

Success is often seen as the accomplishment of a goal or the fulfillment of our desires and aspirations. It varies from person to person, as everyone has different dreams and ambitions. Some individuals perceive success as attaining a specific profession like being a doctor, lawyer, or owning a business. For others, success might mean building a happy family, exploring different parts of the world, or making a positive impact in their community.

The pursuit of success serves as a powerful motivator, pushing us to strive for greatness. However, it's crucial to recognize that success is not universally defined. Each person has their own unique vision of what it means to succeed. What truly matters is defining success according to your own values and aspirations, and then taking steps to accomplish it.

This chapter delves into my personal experiences and reflections on success. It emphasizes the significance of setting clear goals, taking calculated risks, and embracing failure as an opportunity for growth. Moreover, it explores the diverse ways individuals interpret success and provides guidance on discovering your own definition.

It's important to note that the contents of this chapter are based solely on my subjective thoughts and experiences, rather than scientific research. Nevertheless, I hope that by sharing my insights, it can offer you some guidance and support as you embark on your own unique path to success. Remember, success is a journey, and the most fulfilling version of it is one that aligns with your passions and aspirations.

How do you define success?

Is it measured by wealth, status or achievement.

This is something I've considered at length. Did you ever experience success? You might have experienced happiness from your achievements, or delight at your bank balance. But in my view true success can be multifaceted and maybe more complex to gauge.

In my view, and in fact in my experience, success is survival.

Of the many things which can pull you back you from going forwards, our past is definitely prodigious amongst them.

My father had a teashop in my village where, as a school boy, I would go to cover for him during his lunch break. To make the tea he used a manual furnace which I was forbidden to use. He always stopped me from using that furnace so I took my books to the teashop and did my homework.

Since it was lunch time very few people would be there, and those that were only came to read papers or chit chat. But one particular old man used to come everyday and whenever he saw me, he would point and make comments.

"Arey, better not wasting time with books , start learn to make tea"

Then he'd start discussing my reading habit with other customers and make more derogatory comments. After each remark his face would crumple into an awkward, goading smile as he was enjoying his own comments.

This became a routine.

He, became a dreadful chapter in my life. This inconsequential old man and his senseless remarks could easily have been overlooked, but I couldn't. As the days passed, I became phobic of that gnarled old man with his repeating screenplay.

One day, my class teacher asked me to participate in a literature festival. I had never taken part in such literature contests before. All the same I agreed and started preparing for it. And sometimes I prepared from the teashop too.

When the old man came to know about my participation it gave him more cause to laugh at me and more reason to continue his very public denigration of me. He even made a bet with others that I will be eliminated at the very first level.

I participated in three categories, Elocution, Story writing and Poetry writing. When I was at the event I never thought of the friends and teachers who encouraged me, but only of the old man and his nagging insults. But I saw how this was my first chance to finally subjugate him. And so I won. And I won convincingly. With first prized for poetry and story writing and second prize in elocution i was crowned the Sarga Prathibha, overall champion, of the event.

The next day I took the certificates and trophies to the teashop, where I waited for my Goliath. I was ready for him, to talk to him with the eloquent and cutting words of a literary giant. To strike him dead with my fearless diatribe, which, incidentally, I had done a lot of bedroom rehearsals for the previous night.

But, he never came again to the shop. In time I heard that cardiac arrest had brought his demise. Death denied me my glory, or so I thought. But I realised my victory was sweeter. I realised where he died I had survived. Not only in life but I had survived him, his insults, his deprecation but most importantly I survived his will for who I should be.

I had two choices, his will for me to spend my life making tea or mine to prove myself with my creativity and follow my ambition. Making tea seemed easier than winning a competition. One choice was surrendering and other surviving. Choice, not fate, choice is always based on a selection and completely within our own power.

So thereby success is also a choice, and directly proportional to the effort we make. Success can also be a byproduct of the revenge or struggle.

So let me conclude.

Survival is revenge.

Survival is the criteria of the strength we earned.

Survival is the best reply ever you can ever give.

Again, Success and failure are relative terms. What one person considers a success, another person might consider a failure. This is because success is based on our individual goals and desires. What we want to achieve in life will determine what we consider to be successful.

For example, someone who wants to become a doctor might consider it a success to get into medical school. However, someone who wants to be a writer might consider it a success to get their first book published.

The level of our desires also plays a role in our definition of success. If we have low expectations, then we will be more likely to consider ourselves successful even if we achieve relatively small goals. On the other hand, if we have high expectations, then we will need to achieve much larger goals in order to consider ourselves successful.

So, should we let someone else define what our success should look like? The answer is no. Our success is our own to define. No one else can tell us what we should want to achieve in life.

To illustrate this point, imagine that someone else decided what food you should eat. They might tell you that you should only eat healthy foods, even if you don't enjoy them. This would be absurd, because you are the one who has to eat the food. You should be the one who decides what you want to eat.

In the same way, you should be the one who decides what your success should look like. You are the one who has to live your life, so you should be the one who decides what is important to you.

So don't let anyone else define your success for you. Define it for yourself and then go out and achieve it.

CHAPTER 8

A magic wand - Compartmentalization

I build little boxes, neatly in a row,
Each one holding a problem I know.
I tuck them away, like secrets untold,
Protecting my heart, as stories unfold.
In one box, I keep the stress of my work,
Separate from joys, where dreams can lurk.
With focus and purpose, I tackle each task,
Leaving no room for doubts that would bask.

Compartmentalization is a way of dealing with difficult thoughts or feelings by separating them from other parts of your life. We go can through some examples in our day today life.

- A person who works in a high-pressure job might compartmentalize their work stress from their personal life.
- A person who has experienced trauma might compartmentalize the memories of the trauma from their everyday thoughts and feelings.
- A person who is struggling with addiction might compartmentalize their addiction from their other relationships and responsibilities.

When you compartmentalize, it means you mentally separate different thoughts, feelings, or experiences into different boxes in your mind. This can make it easier for you to handle them.

For example, imagine you have a demanding job and a busy personal life. To manage them better, you might put your work-related thoughts and emotions in one box in your mind, and your personal thoughts and emotions in another box. This way, you can focus on each aspect separately without letting them overlap and create confusion.

Another example could be when you encounter a difficult situation or have a problem. You might put your feelings and thoughts about that situation into a separate mental box, so that you can temporarily set them aside and focus on other things in your life.

Sometimes, compartmentalization happens automatically, without you consciously deciding to do it. This can occur when you feel overwhelmed or when you're dealing with a lot of things at once. However, if you notice that you're constantly compartmentalizing, it's important to be aware of the potential negative effects.

Compartmentalization can lead to suppressed emotions, meaning that you might not fully acknowledge or address your feelings. This can prevent you from understanding and processing your emotions in a healthy way. Additionally, relying too much on compartmentalization as a coping mechanism can be unhealthy because it may prevent you from properly dealing with the underlying issues. Lastly, compartmentalization can also cause problems in your relationships, as it can make it difficult to connect with others on a deeper level if you keep parts of your life isolated.

It's important to find a balance between compartmentalizing when needed and also allowing yourself to fully experience and address your emotions and experiences in a healthy and constructive way.

The stress way

Compartmentalization can help reduce stress by providing a psychological mechanism to manage overwhelming thoughts, emotions, and experiences. Scientifically speaking, when we compartmentalize, we engage in a process known as cognitive restructuring.

Cognitive restructuring involves reorganizing and reframing our thoughts and perceptions. By creating mental compartments for different aspects of our lives, we can prioritize and address them individually, rather than allowing them to all blend together and amplify our stress levels. Here's how compartmentalization can help reduce stress from a scientific perspective:

Enhanced focus: When we compartmentalize, we allocate our attention and mental resources to specific areas of concern. By doing so, we can direct our focus and energy toward one task or issue at a time. This concentrated focus helps reduce the cognitive load and prevents us from feeling overwhelmed by trying to deal with everything at once.

Emotional regulation: Compartmentalization allows us to temporarily set aside intense emotions related to specific situations. By segregating these emotions, we create space to regulate and manage them more effectively. This can prevent emotional overload and enable us to approach each challenge with a clearer mindset.

Stress buffering: By mentally separating different aspects of our lives, such as work and personal life, we can establish boundaries and create a sense of control. This sense of control acts as a buffer against stress, as it helps us maintain a balance and prevent one area from excessively affecting others.

Problem-solving efficiency: When we compartmentalize, we can approach problems and challenges one at a time. This enables us to allocate our cognitive resources more efficiently and work through issues in a structured manner. By breaking down complex problems into smaller, more manageable components, we enhance our problem-solving abilities and reduce stress associated with feeling overwhelmed.

However, it's important to note that while compartmentalization can be beneficial for stress reduction, it's not a long-term solution. Regularly relying solely on compartmentalization without addressing underlying issues or emotions can lead to negative consequences in the long run. It's crucial to balance compartmentalization with healthy emotional processing and seeking support when needed.

When dealing with relationships

Compartmentalization in relationships means putting thoughts or feelings about our partner into different boxes in our minds. We do this to deal with conflicts or problems in our relationships. It can be useful in long-term relationships to avoid unnecessary fights over small things. But it can be a problem in the early stages of dating when we should be evaluating if someone is a good fit for us.

When we are getting to know someone, we might find things about them that we don't like. To deal with this discomfort, we might lock away those thoughts or emotions in a box and focus on the positive aspects of the person. Later on, we might realize that we "ignored the red flags" because we actually compartmentalized them.

It's important to note that compartmentalization can happen in all types of relationships, not just romantic ones. Here are some examples:

Disagreeing about politics: If you and your partner have different political views, you might choose not to think about it or avoid discussing politics altogether to maintain a positive relationship.

Disagreeing about friendships: If you disagree with your partner, parents, or friends about whether you should be friends with someone else, you may decide to avoid the topic altogether to prevent conflicts.

Attitudes towards pets: Let's say you've been dating someone for six months and you're starting to fall in love. However, you discover that they are mean to your new dog. In order to stay in the relationship, you might compartmentalize this experience and avoid interactions between your partner and your dog.

While compartmentalizing can provide temporary relief, it's important to address underlying concerns and evaluate whether these issues may have a long-term impact on the relationship. Communication and open discussion are crucial for maintaining healthy relationships where concerns are addressed rather than compartmentalized away.

Here are some additional tips for dealing with compartmentalization in relationships:

- Be honest with yourself about what you are feeling. Don't try to push away your negative thoughts or emotions.
- Talk to your partner about your concerns. Communication is key to any healthy relationship.
- Seek professional help if you need it. A therapist can help you to understand your thoughts and feelings and develop healthy coping mechanisms.

A magic Wand, But Not Aladin's Lamp

Compartmentalizing is a psychological strategy that some individuals use to separate different aspects of their lives. While it can be a helpful tool in certain situations, it can also be observed in individuals engaging in aberrant sexual or social behavior. Let's take a closer look at this phenomenon.

In some cases, individuals who engage in harmful or inappropriate behavior may compartmentalize it from other areas of their life. For example, a boss who sexually harasses their female employees may portray a completely different persona when it comes to their role as a father. They may be loving and caring towards their daughters, creating a stark contrast between their behavior at work and their behavior within their family.

Similarly, someone struggling with substance abuse issues, such as drugs and alcohol, may appear stable and composed when interacting with their parents. They may hide their addictive behavior and maintain a facade of normality, while engaging in harmful habits behind closed doors. This ability to dissociate and separate their behavior allows them to function differently in different areas of their life, concealing their issues from certain individuals or contexts.

The purpose of compartmentalizing in these situations is to maintain a sense of control, protect their image, and avoid confronting the consequences or conflicts that their inappropriate behavior may bring. By mentally separating their actions and emotions, they can continue their harmful behavior while projecting a different persona in other areas of their life.

It's important to note that while compartmentalizing may temporarily serve as a coping mechanism for these individuals, it is not a healthy or sustainable long-term solution. Addressing the underlying issues, seeking help, and promoting open communication are crucial steps towards breaking down these compartments and fostering healthier behavior patterns.

One negative example of compartmentalization in family life is when a parent chooses to ignore or downplay conflicts or issues within the family. They may compartmentalize these problems by avoiding addressing them or pretending that everything is fine. This can lead to unresolved tension and emotional distance within the family unit.

For instance, let's say there is a constant pattern of arguments and disagreements between the parents in a household. Instead of openly discussing and working through these conflicts, one parent may compartmentalize the issues by keeping a "happy family" facade in front of the children. They may avoid acknowledging the problems, dismiss or minimize their impact, and maintain a false sense of harmony.

While this approach may temporarily shield the children from the stress and discomfort of conflict, it creates a disconnect between the reality of the family dynamics and the image that is projected. The children may grow up with a distorted perception of healthy relationships, lacking the necessary skills to navigate conflicts and communicate effectively.

Compartmentalizing family issues in this manner can also prevent necessary interventions and support. By avoiding confrontation and ignoring the underlying problems, the family may miss out on opportunities for growth, healing, and strengthening their bonds.

It's important to note that open and honest communication, addressing conflicts, and seeking professional help when needed are essential for maintaining healthy family relationships. Compartmentalization in this negative sense can hinder the development of a nurturing and supportive family environment.

Understanding and recognizing this pattern of compartmentalization is important in identifying and addressing harmful behavior. By creating awareness, we can encourage individuals to seek appropriate support and work towards integrating their different aspects of life in a more cohesive and positive manner.

If you find yourself compartmentalizing a lot, it's important to be aware of the potential consequences. Compartmentalization can lead to:

Suppressed emotions. When you compartmentalize your emotions, you're not allowing yourself to fully experience them. This can lead to emotional distress, such as anxiety, depression, and anger.

Unhealthy coping mechanisms. If you're not dealing with your difficult thoughts and feelings in a healthy way, you might turn to unhealthy coping mechanisms, such as substance abuse, self-harm, or risky behaviors.

Relationship problems. Compartmentalization can make it difficult to maintain healthy relationships. If you're not sharing your true thoughts and feelings with others, it can be hard to build trust and intimacy.

If you're concerned about your use of compartmentalization, there are things you can do to cope with stress and anxiety in a healthier way. Here are a few tips:

Practice radical acceptance. This means accepting your thoughts and feelings, even the difficult ones. Radical acceptance can help you to stop fighting your emotions and start to heal.

Journal. Writing about your thoughts and feelings can help you to process them in a healthy way.

Seek professional help. If you're struggling to cope with stress and anxiety on your own, talking to a therapist can help. A therapist can teach you healthy coping mechanisms and help you to understand your thoughts and feelings.

If you're concerned about your use of compartmentalization, there are things you can do to cope with stress and anxiety in a healthier way.

CHAPTER 9

We are limited and it is not a problem at all

Let me share with you a tale woven in simple yet enchanting words. Within the pages of this book, I aim to reframe a notion, painting a new picture of the possibilities for an ordinary soul. It is a gentle reminder that nestled within your own boundaries, you still possess the power to conquer almost all your aspirations.

No grandiose volumes of motivation or fervent speeches from charismatic orators are needed. For true confidence arises from a profound connection with reality, where dreams are nurtured by acknowledging one's own strengths and limitations. It is within this realm that persistence finds its voice, whispering words of encouragement and determination.

And as you traverse the path towards your dreams, remember that hard work paves the only road to triumph. Like a diligent artist carefully crafting a masterpiece, each stroke of effort and dedication breathes life into your endeavors. Embrace the challenges that cross your path, for they are the stepping stones on the journey towards achievement. In this narrative, I aspire to illuminate the beauty of embracing one's own limitations while nurturing the seeds of boundless potential.

The study of the mind is a complex and ever-evolving field. We are still learning about how the mind works, and there is much that we do not know. However, one thing that is clear is that the mind is influenced by a variety of factors, including our environment, our experiences, and our genetics.

The environment plays a significant role in shaping our minds. The culture we grow up in, the family we are born into, and the language we speak all influence the way we think and behave. For example, people who grow up in different cultures may have different views on what is considered "normal" or "acceptable" behavior.

Our experiences also play a role in shaping our minds. The things we go through in life, both good and bad, can have a profound impact on our thoughts, feelings, and behaviors. For example, someone who has experienced trauma may be more likely to develop anxiety or depression.

Our genetics also play a role in shaping our minds. Some people are born with a predisposition to certain mental illnesses, such as schizophrenia or autism. However, even if we have a genetic predisposition to a mental illness, our environment and experiences can still play a role in determining whether or not we develop the illness.

It is important to remember that the mind is a complex and dynamic system. It is not something that can be easily understood or controlled. However, by understanding the factors that influence the mind, we can better understand ourselves and others.

In the context of success and failure, it is important to remember that both are a part of life. Everyone experiences success and failure at some point in their lives. However, how we respond to success and failure can have a significant impact on our lives.

If we view success as a destination, we are setting ourselves up for failure. Success is not a destination, it is a journey. It is about continuous learning and improvement. If we focus on the journey, we are more likely to be successful in the long run.

Similarly, if we view failure as a negative event, we are more likely to give up when we fail. Failure is simply a learning opportunity. It is a chance to identify what went wrong and make changes so that we can be successful in the future.

So, remember, you can succeed and fail. Both are a part of life. The important thing is to learn from your experiences and keep moving forward.

Our role models serve as inspiration and guidance, but it's important to remember that they are not extraordinary or superhuman beings. They are ordinary individuals who have accomplished extraordinary feats through their hard work and determination. Despite this reality, the media often portrays them as larger-than-life figures because sensational stories about superhumans capture attention and generate interest.

Unfortunately, this portrayal can create a sense of inadequacy within us. We may feel that our role models are so vastly different from us that we can never reach their level of success. However, this couldn't be further from the truth. Our role models share the same human experiences, fears, doubts, and struggles as we do. The only disparity lies in their unwavering commitment to pursuing their dreams.

To overcome this feeling of inadequacy, it's crucial to identify relatable qualities in our role models. By recognizing that they are just like us, we can gain the confidence to move forward and believe in our own potential. We come to understand that achieving what they have achieved is within our grasp if we put in the necessary effort.

Regrettably, many of us fall into the trap of living in a world of illusions created by the media. We become entranced by the hyperbolic narratives surrounding our role models, perceiving them as superhuman beings. This false perception often leads to us abandoning our own dreams because we believe we can never measure up.

In reality, we possess the capacity to achieve anything we set our minds to. We don't need to possess superhuman qualities to succeed.

All we need is to discover our own unique path in life and relentlessly work towards our goals. It's important not to lose sight of our individuality amidst the illusions and remember that our dreams are attainable through perseverance and staying true to ourselves.

As we reach the conclusion of this book, I want to emphasize the importance of understanding that success is not a one-size-fits-all concept. It is crucial to recognize that defining success is a deeply personal endeavor. What truly matters is that you take ownership of your own definition of success and demonstrate the willingness to put in the necessary effort to achieve it.

When crafting your own definition of success, there are various factors to consider. Your aspirations, skills, abilities, long-term goals, and the progress you have made thus far all play a role. However, the most significant factor in measuring success is your effort.

Effort stands as the true gauge of success and failure. By working diligently and giving your utmost dedication, you can take pride in your accomplishments, even if you do not reach every single goal you have set.

Moreover, it is vital to understand that there is no such thing as "Waste of work." There is simply work. While certain tasks may prove more challenging than others, each task holds equal importance. To attain success, you must embrace a willingness to tackle all tasks, regardless of their perceived difficulty.

So, what criteria will you utilize to define your success? That decision lies solely in your hands. Yet, whatever criteria you choose, ensure that you possess the resolve to put in the hard work required to achieve your goals.

It is important to remember that success does not hinge on attaining perfection. Rather, it is a journey of progress and learning from your mistakes. If you demonstrate a commitment to putting in the work, there is no limit to what you can achieve.

I sincerely hope that this book has inspired you to craft your own definition of success and has instilled in you the drive to work diligently towards your goals. May you embark on your journey with determination and fortune on your side. Good luck!

About the Author

Praveen Vattapparambath is a IT project manager with over 17 years of industry experience. However, his passion lies in the field of psychology, where he has excelled as a dedicated researcher and scholar. With a Master's degree in applied psychology, Praveen brings a unique blend of practical knowledge and academic expertise to his writing.

Driven by an insatiable curiosity about the human mind and behavior, Praveen embarked on a parallel journey as a research scholar in psychology. This endeavor allowed him to delve deeper into the intricacies of the human psyche, exploring various theories, methodologies, and applications within the field. His rigorous academic training combined with his real-world project management experience enables him to provide a unique perspective on the intersection of psychology and practicality.